BOOKWORMS

Animal Builders

A Beaver's Lodge

Erika de Nijs

Cavendish Square

New York

Published in 2017 by Cavendish Square Publishing, LLC
243 5th Avenue, Suite 136, New York, NY 10016

Library of Congress Cataloging-in-Publication Data

Names: de Nijs, Erika.
Title: A beaver's lodge / Erika de Nijs.
Description: New York : Cavendish Square, 2017. | Series: Animal builders| Includes index.
Identifiers: ISBN 9781502620675 (pbk.) | ISBN 9781502620699 (library bound) | ISBN 9781502620682 (6 pack) | ISBN 9781502620705 (ebook)
Subjects: LCSH: Beavers--Juvenile literature. | Beavers--Habitations--Juvenile literature.
Classification: LCC QL737.R632 D38 2017 | DDC 599.37--dc23

Editorial Director: David McNamara
Editor: Fletcher Doyle
Copy Editor: Rebecca Rohan
Assistant Art Director: Amy Greenan
Designer: Stephanie Flecha
Production Coordinator: Karol Szymczuk
Photo Research: J8 Media

The photographs in this book are used by permission and through the courtesy of:

Cover George Lepp/Getty Images; p. 5 Jason Kasumovic/Shutterstock.com; p. 7 Chiswick Chap/uncropped image Marcin Klapczynski/File:American Beaver with dam.JPG/Wikimedia Commons; p. 9 Dorling Kindersley/Thinkstock.com; p. 11 Dominique Braud/Animals Animals; p. 13 Procy/Shutterstock.com; p. 15 UbjsP/Shutterstock.com; p. 17 LesPalenik/Shutterstock.com; p. 19 Ardea/Elizabeth Bomford/Animals Animals; p. 21 Leonard Rue Enterprises/Animals Animals.

Printed in the United States of America

Contents

Beavers stay **busy**.
They work hard.

4

5

Beavers build dams.
Beavers build **lodges**.

Beavers live in the lodges.
Lodges have many rooms.

The lodge door is **underwater**. This keeps beavers safe.

11

Beavers cut down trees.
They use their teeth.

13

Beavers have big families.
They live in one lodge.

15

Lodges have thick walls.
The beavers stay warm
inside.

Lodges have an **airhole**. This lets in air for beavers to breathe.

Beavers can fix dams.
They are great builders.

21

New Words

airhole (EHR-hohl) A hole that lets in air.

busy (BI-zee) Always doing work.

dam (DAM) A barrier that stops the flow of a river or a stream.

lodges (LAHJ-ez) Homes for animals like beavers.

underwater (uhn-dur-WAH-tur) Down below the water's surface.

Index

About the Author

Erika de Nijs played college hockey before becoming a teacher and a writer. Her parents are from the Netherlands, but she was raised in upstate New York, where there are many beavers.

About BOOKWORMS

Bookworms help independent readers gain reading confidence through high-frequency words, simple sentences, and strong picture/text support. Each book explores a concept that helps children relate what they read to the world they live in.